WOLFF & BYRD

COUNSELORS OF THE MACABRE

by Batton Lash

SUPERNATURAL LAW

SIDEBAR BOOKS

New York

All the stories in this book originally appeared in *The National Law Journal* except for "Nine Points of the Law" and "The Gawdawful Thing," which originally appeared in *American Fantasy* magazine. "Lawyers in Hell" originally appeared in *The Brooklyn Paper*.

Any similarities between any of the the names, characters, and places depicted in the stories in this book with those of any living or dead persons or institutions is purely coincidental.

All stories lettered by Rick Parker. "Supernatural Law" cover logo designed by John Workman. Typesetting by Jackie Estrada. Production by Dave Estrada and Steve Smith. Cover color by Clydene Nee of In Color.

Acknowledgments

Sincere thanks to: Doreen Weisenhaus, Tim Robinson, Doug Hunt, Rosemary Olander, Deidre Leipziger, Joseph Phalon, and Marc Desmond of *The National Law Journal;* Ed Weintrob, Ann V. Bollinger, Paul Toomey, Allison Guercio, and Margaret Daly of Brooklyn Paper Publications; Bob and Nancy Garcia of *American Fantasy;* Russell Calabrese for his design of the plaintiff in "Wonky, the Wonderful Widdle Cat"; Libby Harrison, Ray Deter, and Avery Eli Okin for the legal research; Michael and Janet Gilbert; Susan Grode; Mitch Berger, Esq.; and, of course, my family: Mom, Dad, Irene, Billy, Nancy, and Mary.

I would especially like to thank Sandy Hausler, Jami Bernard, and Jackie Estrada, without whom this book would not have been possible.

—B.L.

**THIS BOOK IS DEDICATED TO
JACKIE ESTRADA**

Exhibit A Press
4657 Cajon
San Diego, CA 92115

Printed in the United States of America
First edition
5 4 3 2 1

ISBN 0-9633954-0-8

THE DOCKET

FOREWORD

Monsters! I hate 'em!

Lawyers! I hate 'em!

I know, you've heard those words a million times before. Maybe you've even said 'em yourself. I know I have. Still, if there were ever two unfairly maligned segments of society, lawyers and monsters are it!

Sure, monsters can be frisky! So maybe they chew the brainstem off some whiny lab assistant on occasion! Everyone's entitled to one bad day, right? And considering all the dumb cheerleaders and stupid jocks that monsters dispose of, we should thank them for chlorinating our collective gene pool!

And *lawyers*? Okay, they occasionally bend the rules a smidge. Hey, they're only *human*! For a few extra billing hours, some'll even turn a friendly divorce into a Stephen King bloodbath! Then there're those guys who love to get those lousy, stinkin' mass murderers off on goddamn technicalities. And what about those @#$%&! fat cat corporate lawyers who shovel PAC money down the throats of their slimy politician buddies so some chemical company can crap toxic waste on the rest of us! What about that, huh? You @#$%&! leaches! You lyin' sacks of . . . ahem . . . *cough*

As I was saying, if there was ever an unfairly maligned segment of our population, monsters are it!

But don't cry, monsters! Dry your tears, lawyers! Hold those defamation of character suits, boys . . . Batton Lash is on the case!

Yes, *the* Batton Lash! The guy who created Wolff & Byrd for the *Brooklyn Paper* way back in 1979. The guy who stole the thunder from my own character, Mr. Monster! Yes . . . *that* guy!

You see, years ago, when I started drawing Mr. Monster, I thought I had a pretty good gimmick: a monster-fighting superhero. Leave it to Bat to do me one better. He created a pair of sharp, honest lawyers (yeah, *right!*) that *defend* monsters! Are we working at cross purposes, or what?

His creations, on the other hand, work very well together indeed. Alanna Wolff and Jeffrey Byrd are partners in every sense of the word. Wolff is a smart, dynamic, and feminine legal eagle, ably backed up by Byrd, the patient workhorse of the team. Wolff and Byrd like and respect each other. That's unusual enough in real life, but rarer than Congressional ethics in the funny pages!

By making Wolff and Byrd friends, rather than lovers, Bat has mercifully saved the long-suffering comic strip fan from the eternal "poor-nurse-mooning-over-handsome-unattainable-doctor" soap opera scenario. And I can't thank him enough for that!

So who is Batton Lash, anyway? To the casual observer, he's a nice Italian boy, the kind of skinny kid any mother would gladly urge, "Mangia, mangia!" A battle-scarred New Yorker, Bat can often be found creating cartoon magic in the tiny rent-controlled closet he calls home. Ever the perfectionist, this "Sultan of Sweat" never lets a page out of his hands until he's reworked it to his satisfaction. His Catholic guilt won't let him do a *good* job; he's got to bleed ink on each page or he feels he's cheating the reader. And Batton's too honest a guy to ever do that!

Fortunately for Wolff & Byrd, Bat's obsessive search for just the right phrase or camera angle hasn't stifled his brilliant flights of fancy one bit. Who else but Brooklyn's "Italian Scallion" could come up with concepts as weird as a vampire dentist or as clever as a tax collector from the future?

Beyond Bat's engaging characters and his wickedly clever plots, the first thing that strikes the casual Wolff & Byrd reader is the strip's sheer density. No, strike that! Wolff & Byrd has no casual readers! There's too much in each panel for that! As I see it, Bat figures that if he's going to kill himself writing and drawing the very best strip he can, the least we readers can do is take the time and effort to read it!

Luckily, the effort is well worth it. Beyond Bat's clever wordplay and striking artwork, a crazy quilt of insane, brilliant, funny ideas are stacked like a jury in each strip. Who but Bat would have the audacity to mix monsters and lawyers in a comic strip . . . and make it work?

Actually, his skill and imagination aren't too surprising, if you look at his artistic influences. Bat studied under two genuine cartoon geniuses: Golden Age great Will Eisner and the original creator of *Mad* magazine, Harvey Kurtzman. Looking at the strips reprinted in this volume, one can see traces of Kurtzman's irreverent humor and barbed satire that inspired a generation of *Mad* fans to grow up to become lazy, cynical, smartmouthed hippies! Swell idol you've got there, pal! Wolff & Byrd's inventive panel layouts and continual visual experimentation come courtesy of Eisner's classic 1940s comic strip, *The Spirit*. Additionally, Spider-Man co-creator Steve Ditko's influence can be felt in the strange spooks, spacemen, and assorted weirdos that populate Wolff & Byrd.

The crazy ideas are all Bat's though—as well as the terrible puns! As a result, we wind up with stories like the one where Clarence Darrow's ghost takes over the body of a young trial lawyer. Or how about the client who drives Wolff and Byrd crazy . . . in a haunted mobile home no less? Or even the time Wolff and Byrd defended my old pal Mr. Monster against a particularly litigious space creature? Whew! That's one I owe you, Bat!

But enough talking! It's time to start reading. When you're through, maybe you'll still say:

Monsters, I hate 'em!

Lawyers, I hate 'em!

But put 'em together, and you've got Wolff & Byrd.

And them you just gotta love!

Michael T. Gilbert
Eugene, Oregon, 1992

Michael T. Gilbert's Mr. Monster comics, published by Tundra, are available at comics specialty shops everywhere.

NINE POINTS OF THE LAW

THE
Rock 'N' Holy
Roller

7

The Invasion of the Law Firm Snatchers

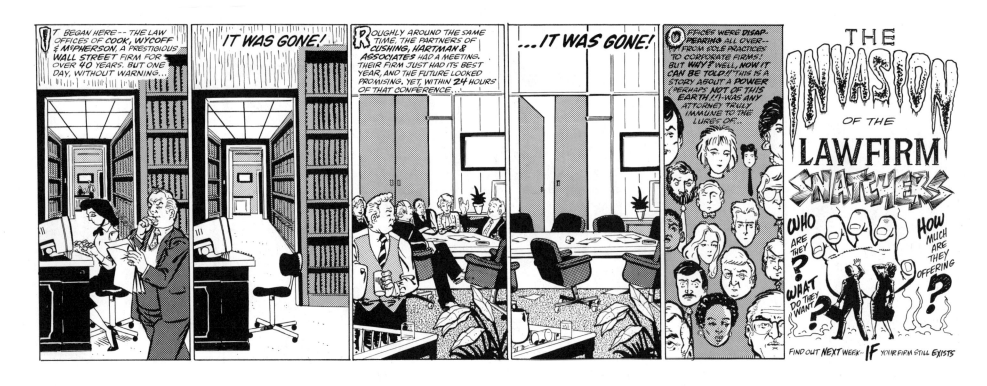

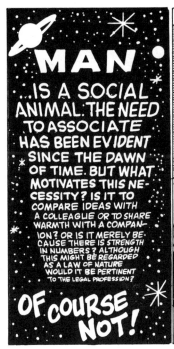

GAWDAWFUL THING

(An American Folk-Law)

WOLFF & BYRD
COUNSELORS
of the
MACABRE

Words & Pictures:
BATTON LASH
Music:
TRADITIONAL

Hear Ye, Hear Ye! This here song's 'bout a brute who meant no wrong

It was big 'n ugly, that's no lie — but heck, It wouldn't hurt a fly

It was all the news, this thing that oozed — with colors of green & brown

ARTIST'S RENDERING

SATAN RISES FROM SWAMP

The day It threw caution to the wind — and clambered into town.

Oh, It shambled and stank, from where it's dark and dank / There's no need for alarm -- It don't mean you no harm. Judge for yourself in this story I sing, the tale of the pitiful poor GAWDAWFUL thing.

RETURN OF THE THING
$1 AT ALL TIMES

RISING FAWN GROCERY

Nobody cottoned to this fella from the swamp

Fact is, a mob was formed pretty prompt.

Gathering by their hateful stares, the beast thought "Nobody cares!"

But Its defenders came out of the dark (this kinda situation's how they made their mark)

When they spoke, the rabble shook at the knees— they learned they violated the creature's Civil Liberties!

Oh, it shambled and stank, but a complaint it made frank / The freak they sought wants to take 'em to court! Who knows what the future will bring— when you're sued by a GAWDAWFUL thing?

14

Well, folks got ornery-- an' downright rude (they knew attorneys were awfully shrewd)

'Cause, in addition to chargin' some rednecks with assault the lawyers found the town's ethics at fault.

Seemed nobody gave a hoot where they dumped toxic waste Shoot! 'Fore long, that ol' swamp was chemically laced.

An Environmentalist made the township perspire-- heard tell, he went into the mire!

Oh, it bubbled and stank; he groped but he sank Nobody came-- it was a cryin' shame.

But who's that testifying against the evil ring?

The EPA man, that's who-- why, HE'S the GAWDAWFUL thing!

It took the stand, dripping with slime
(day after day, too — these — things take time)

The counselors were called to the bench
"Let's wrap this up — the court can't take the stench"

"Your honor, malfeasance made our client a walking mess; compensation is due for Its emotional distress!"

A mistrial's what the town's lawyer tried to arrange — but that was overruled when the proceedings really got strange

Oh, they shambled and stank and faces went blank; The vigilantes all mutated — y'see — they got contaminated!
There'll be action now with some tails in a sling / Tsk! This could'a been avoided, too... THAT'S really the GAWDAWFUL thing!

DON'T TELL ME, BYRD... POETIC JUSTICE?

IT'S A MONSTER ON THE CHARTS, WOLFF

INFERNAL INTERN

Wonky,
The Wonderful
Widdle Cat

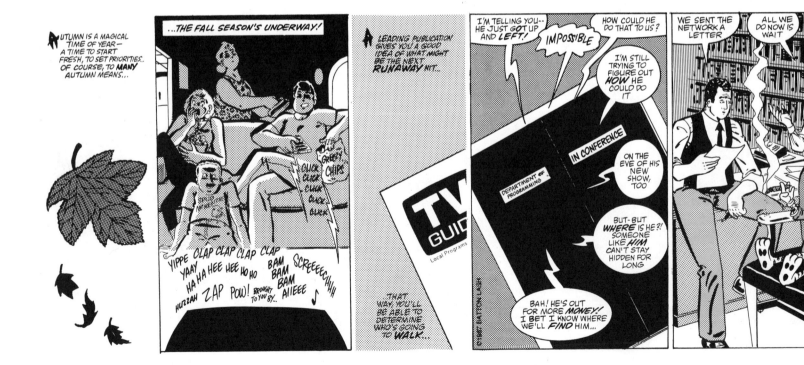

The Haunting

THE BOOGEYMAN

CHANGE OF VENUE

THE
ONCE AND FUTURE
LAWSUIT

ATTORNEYS HAVE FOUGHT FOR *AND* AGAINST THE **XERXES**® CORPORATION FOR YEARS... BUT EVERY SO OFTEN, ESPECIALLY WHEN A NEW LEGAL TAG TEAM JOINS THE FRAY, THE INEVITABLE QUESTION IS RAISED...

ANTI-TRUST VIOLATIONS

FEDERAL SECURITIES

UNCONSTITUTIONAL

UNETHICAL

ILLEGAL SEIZURES

I'VE DRAFTED A MEMO

WE DON'T SHARE OUR SHARES

TENDER OFFER

I'VE DRAFTED A LETTER

OH YEAH?

YEAH!

JUST WHAT THE HECK IS THIS CASE ALL ABOUT?! WELL, BELIEVE IT OR NOT, THIS LEGENDARY LITIGATION BEGAN WITH A **LEGEND**...

The Once and Future Lawsuit

ARTHUR WAS OUTRAGED. "WHAT ARMY COULD CONQUER CAMELOT?"

MERLIN, THE COURT COUNSELOR, ATTEMPTED TO EXPLAIN HIS GRIM VISION TO THE KING.

"A GREAT BATTLE WILL COME TO PASS WHERE NO BLOOD IS SHED, BUT TAKEOVER WILL BE HOSTILE... KNIGHTS DRESSED IN EXPENSIVE CLOTHS AND ARMED WITH WRITING STICKS WILL FIGHT FOR POSSESSION OF YOUR CASTLE!"

CURIOSITY PIQUED, THE KING LEANED FORWARD.

"PRAY TELL ME, WILL ANY HEED ARTHUR'S **LAW?**"

THE SORCERER SIGHED. "**MUCH** TALK WILL BE MADE OF **THE** LAW, SIRE... AND **EVERY** WORD UTTERED OR WRITTEN BY THE KNIGHTS' AND THEIR LEADERS' WILL HAVE A TOLL ATTACHED TO IT! THE STRUGGLE WILL GO ON FOR YEARS..."

THE KING WAS CONFUSED. HE DISMISSED THE MAGICIAN TO PONDER HIS STRANGE PROPHECY.

THE FAIR GWYNEVERE SAW THE CONCERN ON HER KING'S FACE.

"IMAGINE! A TIME WILL COME WHEN TAKEOVERS WILL BE HOSTILE BUT BLOODLESS, YET ARGUMENTS WILL HAVE A TARIFF ATTACHED TO THEM." THE KING SHRUGGED. "AND TO THINK, WE JUST GOT **OUT** OF THE DARK AGES!"

NEXT WEEK: Legal Wizardry

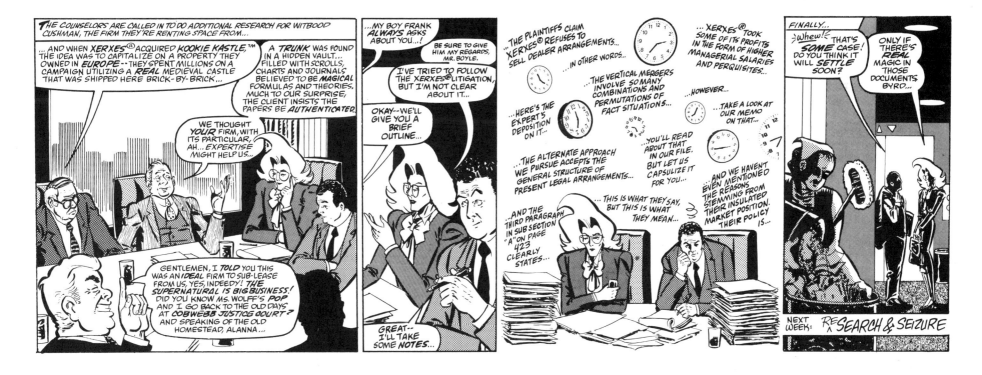

LAWYERS IN HELL

REMEMBER LAST YEAR WHEN REPUTED MOB LEADER **TONY 'DON JUAN' DANTE** WAS INDICTED ON FEDERAL RACKETEERING AND CONSPIRACY CHARGES? DANTE WAS AN IMPECCABLE DRESSER, WOMANIZER AND SHARP BUSINESSMAN (HIS COMPANY, **GOOD INTENTION CONCRETE**, ALWAYS SANK THE COMPETITION).

...MY CLIENT IS INNOCENT! THEY HAVEN'T GOT A CASE!

MR. DANTE--

DON JUAN

C'MON TONY JUST A QUOTE

TONY OVER HERE

YO! DON!

JUST DO THE RIGHT THING

SMILE, TONY.

YESSIR

BUT WHEN IT CAME TO TONY DANTE, JUSTICE WASN'T **SERVED**, SHE HELPED HERSELF...

MOB BIG DRAGGED TO HELL

A packed courtroom recoiled in horror yesterday when the usually demure statue of blind justice strode blithely into the mob trial of Tony (Don Juan) Dante and hurled the cowering defendant into hell, just moments before the jury was to deliver its verdict.

Dante's attorney, a shaken Virgil LePorello, had no comment on this bizarre and unprecedented action, but shocked onlookers reported that the attractive statue was heard to say, "I may be blind, but I can smell trouble--and *this* guy's trouble!" The seven-woman, five-man jury had just concluded five hours of delibe...

© 1988 BATTON LASH

CASE CLOSED? DANTE'S, AH, ASSOCIATES DIDN'T SEE IT THAT WAY...

GET TONY BACK.

BUT--HE-HE'S **DOWN THERE** NOW

HE'S STILL ALIVE, AIN'T HE?

THE VERDICT WASN'T IN-- THAT MEANS HE'S INNOCENT, RIGHT?

TECHNICALLY, YES...

YER A LAWYER-- STRAIGHTEN IT OUT

YESSIR

JUST DO THE RIGHT THING

NESTLED IN HIS EXPENSIVE PARK AVENUE LAW FIRM, VIRGIL LePORELLO WASTES NO TIME. HE DOES WHAT ANY OTHER HIGH-POWERED ATTORNEY MIGHT DO IN HIS SITUATION...

--RETAINS ANOTHER FIRM AS CO-COUNSEL...

VIRGIL LePORELLO? I ALWAYS THOUGHT IT'D BE A **COLD DAY IN HELL** BEFORE A BIGSHOT LIKE **HIM** ASKED FOR OUR HELP!

THEN YOU BETTER PACK A **SWEATER**, BYRD...

WOLFF & BYRD COUNSELORS OF THE MACABRE

NEXT WEEK: *THE BURNING QUESTIONS*

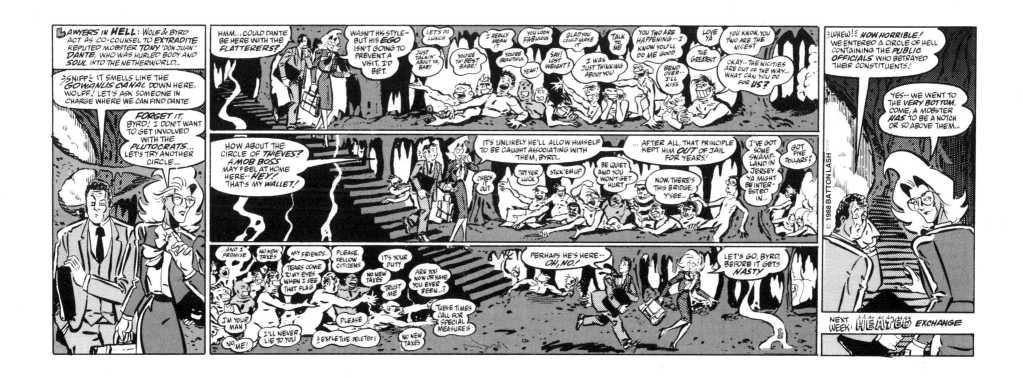

Interim

(I)

WOLFF GOES HOME

52

Byrd and the Brain

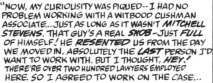

57

59

INTERIM

(II)

Beauty and the Breach

OUR MODERN FABLE CONTINUES: The Beast enters the surface world in broad daylight to court his Beauty... in court...

OH, KATHERINE... KATHERINE! FORGIVE ME FOR WHAT I WILL DO... BUT I MUST LISTEN TO THE PASSION WITHIN MY *HEART*...

© 1989 BATTON LASH

... EVEN THOUGH THE COMMON SENSE IN MY *HEAD* TELLS ME OTHER-WISE...

As the Beast wades his way towards the court-house, tension mounts moments before the trial commences...

HEY-- NICE TO SEE YA, COUNSELOR-- DON'T BOTHER SITTING-- THE JUDGE'LL BE OUT ANY MINUTE NOW

ALL RIGHT, MR. PRINTZ-- I'M *LATE*, SORRY!

HUH. MAYBE IF I HAD *FRANK* SIT IN ON THIS CASE, IT MIGHT'VE GIVEN YOU THE INCENTIVE TO BE HERE ON TIME

THAT WAS UNCALLED FOR, BYRD. I'VE GIVEN *PLENTY* OF MY OWN TIME TO THIS FIRM AND YOU KNOW IT!

NO QUESTION, WOLFF-- BUT I'VE BEEN CARRYING THE BULK OF THE WORK LATELY WHILE YOU'VE BEEN THE DIAL-A-DATE POSTER CHILD!

OH, COME ON NOW--

HEY, GUYS...

...YOU'RE SUPPOSED TO BE ARGUING *MY* CASE, REMEMBER?

ALL RISE...

As the court comes to order, the prosecuting attorney delivers her opening remarks. She makes her case clear: She demands justice. She urges decency. She stresses punitive measures while the jury is held rapt and the state is tickled pink by her purple approach...

INTERESTING-- I'VE NEVER SEEN THE DEATH SCENE FROM *CAMILLE* INTERPRETED IN A COURTROOM BEFORE...

IF YOU *READ* MY MEMO ABOUT KATHERINE HAMMETT YOU WOULD'VE BEEN PREPARED FOR IT

I *READ* YOUR MEMO WHICH WAS SO CONVO-LUTED IT TOOK ME *HOURS* TO PLOW THROUGH

CONVOLUTED?! AT LEAST I DON'T DASH OFF LITTLE NOTES AND CLAIM THEY'RE MEMOS!

≥SIGH≤ I'LL GLADLY *LISTEN* TO WHATEVER MY LAWYERS HAVE TO TELL ME... *IF* I UNDERSTOOD WHAT THEY'RE SAYING THROUGH THEIR *TEETH!*

NEXT WEEK: Separate Opinions

A LEGAL FAIRY TALE CONTINUES: The defense make their play after Beauty's Courtroom theatrics...

I KNEW VICIOUS ROOMERS WOULD DO ME IN, MR. BYRD

IT'S FAR FROM OVER, MR. PRINTZ. LET'S HEAR YOUR SUPERINTENDENT'S TESTIMONY. BEFORE WE TALKED TO HIM, WE WERE WORKING IN A VACUUM!

"REPTILE" LANDLORD TRIAL TODAY

I WANT YOU TO TELL THE COURT, MR. SILSBY...

...EXACTLY WHAT YOU SAW THAT DAY YOU WERE CLEANING THE BASEMENT IN MR. PRINTZ' BUILDING ON KOSLOW STREET

A BIG,,, FURRY,... *THING,* LOOKED LIKE AN *ANIMAL*... BUT IT STOOD UP LIKE A *MAN,* CROSS-EYED, TOO, FRIGHTENED ME-- UNTIL I TOOK A WHACK AT IT! THEN I FELT BAD-- IT RAN OFF LIKE A SCARED CAT!

1989 BATTON LASH

AND *THIS* IS WHAT YOU USED TO DEFEND YOURSELF?

SWUNG IT RIGHT AT 'IM!

The Beauty knows of who they speak; to hear of others learning of the Beast's existence puts her ill at ease...

DAMN! CLARENCE NEVER TOLD ME THE SUPER TOOK A SWAT AT HIM! WHAT'S THAT MANGY LOVER TRYING TO DO-- *RUIN* MY CAREER?!

THAT CLARENCE! A PROSECUTING ATTORNEY SHOULD ALWAYS HAVE A LOVESICK MONSTER THAT LIVES IN THE SEWERS AT HER DISPOSAL-- BUT IS IT *WORTH* IT?! HIS CONSTANT PINING, THOSE AWFUL *POEMS* AND WHAT IT COSTS ME IN *DRY CLEANING!* AND WHO KNOWS HOW MUCH LONGER I CAN HOLD HIM *OFF?* HE'S QUITE ROMANTIC FOR A *BEAST,* BUT FACE IT-- HE'S AN *ANIMAL* LIKE ANY OTHER GUY...

BUT I'M NOT WORRIED, CLARENCE WOULD DO *ANYTHING* FOR ME. ESPECIALLY WHEN IT COMES TO *DISCOURAGING* MY ADVERSARIES. STILL, I HOPE HE'S LITTLE MORE DEMONSTRATIVE WITH *THESE* ATTORNEYS...

...AND IN YOUR OPINION, MR. SILSBY, WHY DO YOU THINK THIS... MAN-BEAST CHOSE MR. PRINTZ' BUILDING OUT OF ALL THE BUILDINGS ON KOSLOW STREET?

HEY, THESE ARE *TOUGH* TIMES...

...A THING THAT LOOKS LIKE *THAT* WAS PROBABLY JUST LOOKING FOR A PLACE TO *CRASH!*

CREEEEEEAKKKK

NEXT WEEK: LOWERING THE BOOM

67

Summation

BATTON LASH was born and raised in Brooklyn, New York. He attended James Madison High School in Brooklyn and the School of Visual Arts in Manhattan. After graduating from Visual Arts (where his instructors included Will Eisner and Harvey Kurtzman), Lash went to work as an artist and copywriter for a small-time advertising agency. During this period he also did freelance illustrations for such clients as Waldenbooks, Simon & Schuster, the *New York Daily News*, *Women's World*, and Murder to Go and for the book *Rock 'n' Roll Confidential*. When in 1979 Brooklyn Paper Publications asked him to create a comic strip, Lash came up with "Wolff & Byrd, Counselors of the Macabre," and it has been running in the local weekly newspapers ever since. The *National Law Journal* has featured the strip since 1983. Wolff & Byrd stories have appeared in a number of comic books, including *Mr. Monster, Munden's Bar, Frankie's Frightmare*, and *Panorama*, and "Wolff & Byrd" is also a regular feature in TSR's *Polyhedron Newszine* and in the *Comics Buyer's Guide*. Batton Lash finds himself surrounded by hundreds of lawyers since he resides a few blocks from the courts in downtown Brooklyn.